Frogs and toads of th...

597 SIM

W9-CFH-434

Simon, Hilda.

Elisabeth C Adams MiddleSchool

FROGS and TOADS
of the world

FROGS

and TOADS

of the world

Written and Illustrated by

Hilda Simon

J.B. Lippincott Company   Philadelphia and New York

COPYRIGHT © 1975 BY HILDA SIMON

ALL RIGHTS RESERVED

PRINTED IN THE UNITED STATES OF AMERICA

FIRST EDITION

597
S

U.S. Library of Congress Cataloging in Publication Data

Simon, Hilda.
  Frogs and toads of the world.

  Bibliography: p.
  Includes index.
  SUMMARY: Describes the physical characteristics, habits, and natural
environment of various frogs and toads.
  1. Frogs—Juvenile literature. 2. Toads—Juvenile literature. [1. Frogs. 2. Toads]
I. Title.
QL668.EaS55   597'.8   75-14095
ISBN-0-397-31634-8

ADAMS MIDDLE SCHOOL LIBRARY GUILFORD

Contents

List of Illustrations

Of Frogs and Man

Fairy tales frequently indicate popular beliefs and superstitions, especially when their roots are very old and can be traced to ancient folktale sources. In most fairy tales in which frogs appear—such as the well-known story of the Frog Prince—they are cast in benevolent roles, often as humans in disguise, whereas their close relatives the toads usually represent something evil or sinister. Thus toads were almost invariably a prominent ingredient of witches' brews, and during the Inquisition, when witch-hunts and trials were at their height, a toad found in the vicinity of a woman suspected of witchcraft was often all the "evidence" needed to tip the scales against her. Needless to say, this fact could be, and frequently was, exploited by people wanting to get rid of others for their own shady reasons.

The superstitions attached to toads have been slow to disappear. Even today there are people who believe that a person can get warts from touching the skin of a toad. In woeful ignorance of the indispensable role played by these amphibians in the control of a wide range of plant-destroying pests, farmers in many countries for centuries exterminated these useful creatures wherever they encountered them, thereby killing off their own allies.

In searching for the reasons for such misconceptions and prejudice, we find that the most important one seems to be the toads' appearance, closely followed by their habits. It is unfortunate that being attractive is frequently more than half the battle in winning acceptance, regardless of "inner worth." The homely individual has a much tougher time. Even the toads' best friends are forced to admit that toads, by and large, are rather homely if not to say ugly with their squat, chunky bodies, their wart-covered skin, their usually somber colors. Except for their eyes, which are large and really quite beautiful, toads are physically unattractive. Along with this must be considered the fact that since they are mainly nocturnal animals, their slug and insect hunting is done at night when no one sees them. They spend much of the day hidden away in holes, crevices, and burrows where to the casual observer they seem to be doing nothing useful.

In comparison, most frogs are gay cavaliers. Active by day—the night is usually reserved for musical offerings, especially during breeding time—frogs enjoy light and sun. A green frog sitting on a lily pad in a pond, its smooth skin glistening, its large eyes bright as they watch for any flying insect that may venture too close, is the very picture of open, satisfied, happy enjoyment of life, and one with which the much more secretive toads cannot compete.

To what extent prejudices against toads have become part and parcel of popular thinking is best demonstrated by the way their name is used. In several languages, including English and German, *toad* is a contemptuous term for an ugly or unpleasant person. The English dictionary definition for toad in this sense is "a hateful person or thing," and to toady means to crawl or to fawn upon someone wealthy or powerful.

All this should not be taken to mean that frogs have been exempt from depredation by man—what wildlife ever has been? However, the reason for killing frogs has not been superstition or ignorance. If anything, frogs have been hunted because they became *too* well known. The long, fleshy hind legs of larger frogs have been appreciated as tasty morsels since ancient times. Very old records describe them as delicacies served at the dinner tables of the wealthy. People learned very early to take advantage of adding to their diets animals that could not fight back and were relatively easy to capture.

In the past century, frogs became objects of scientific experimentation, resulting in the slaughter of uncounted millions. They have been decapitated, dismembered, and otherwise mutilated in the course of research projects. This depredation continues today, and because they are considered "lower" animals and therefore deemed incapable of feelings, they frequently are not given even the most rudimentary consideration by experimenters eager to discover new biological and medical facts. Thus we have a mass of anatomical information accumulated over the years through the study of dead frogs, but there is comparatively little known about how frogs conduct their lives.

Today, as a result of a surge of interest in animal behavior, many more naturalists are studying live frogs and toads in an effort to find out about their habits, relative intelligence, and behavior patterns. Observation of the "pet" frog, an area left mainly to children in the past, has become a part of the overall inquiry into animal behavior. Certain facts, such as the apparently somewhat higher level of intelligence of toads as compared to that of frogs, have resulted from these studies, but there is still a great deal that is unknown, or incompletely known, even about some familiar species. Anyone who has ever kept frogs and toads in captivity, and has devoted the time, patience, and sympathetic understanding necessary to observe, tame, and train them, knows that individuals even of the same species may display great differences in disposition, temperament, and "character." Such studies therefore are a rich field for new discoveries by amateur and professional naturalists alike, especially because frogs are easy to obtain and easy to keep.

I have had extensive experience in keeping frogs and toads as pets, often raising them from eggs and watching them change and grow into adults. I have nursed wounded frogs back to health and observed their amazing powers of regenerating badly damaged parts of their bodies. Most of these animals I remember only as representatives of their group—tree frogs, grass frogs, toads—but a few remain in my mind as distinct individuals.

When I was a child in Europe I had a frog called Emil who was beloved by my entire family. He was an eminently sensible frog, and was content to sit quietly on my desk beside my school books while I was doing my homework. He especially liked to be carried around on my palm, which he undoubtedly enjoyed because quite often I let him catch a few fat flies at the kitchen window. Emil lived with us until he was fully grown, when I released him to live a life in the wild.

Then more recently there was Max, an American green frog. I originally acquired Max while writing a book on chameleons and other animals, including amphibians, that can change their colors and patterns, because I wanted to compare the ability of various amphibians to affect such changes. Max became much more than a subject to be observed, however. He was an obvious extrovert and had something to say about everything. The sound of conversation animated him to join in with loud and persistent croaking. It quickly became evident that he was able to tell my voice from any other, as he would greet me happily in the morning as soon as he heard me speak, but not respond to anyone else.

Max and Emil were unforgettable personalities whose behavior was much more intelligent than is generally associated with amphibians. They, and several others I have known personally, have given me insights into their life-styles that I found invaluable in my research for this book.

In the chapters that follow, we will meet a great many frogs and toads from around the world: the large and the small, the homely and the handsome, the clumsy and the acrobatic. Among them are some that are fully aquatic, others that prefer to live underground, and still others with "lofty" habits that spend their entire lives high up in the trees. Many need the moist, steaming heat of tropical jungles to survive. At the other end of the scale, a few have chosen as their habitat the rough, inimical climate of steep mountain slopes at high altitudes. Some are fascinating; all are interesting for the proof they offer of the tremendous variety of life-styles that has made the tailless amphibians so successful and widespread a group.

1 Evolution, Anatomy, and Metamorphosis

The earliest ancestors of the amphibians—animals that can lead a "double life"—are assumed to have crawled out of the water and onto dry land more than 300 million years ago and so started all the terrestrial, air-breathing animal groups. We do not know what prompted these ancient creatures to leave their native habitat and venture ashore for an existence of unprecedented challenges, although there are several theories that attempt an explanation. One theory suggests that severe droughts reduced the water level, especially in shallow coastal areas, and forced a different life-style on the inhabitants of those regions. Or the change may have been voluntary. The peculiar behavior of mudskippers of tropical coastal regions, small fish that like to leave the water and use their pectoral fins to hop around on muddy ground, would seem to indicate that changes in living habits may occur without drastically altered environmental conditions.

In any case, the earliest amphibians must have looked somewhat like fish on legs: clumsy, awkward, breathing air

Eryops, *a fossil amphibian.*

only with difficulty, but all the same surviving and moving around on land.

We assume that one group of descendants from these earliest ancestors succeeded relatively soon in breaking all ties to a water-bound existence and becoming purely terrestrial; another, from which the modern amphibians derived, never completely lost their need to spend at least part of their lives in the water. Thus most amphibians have a free-swimming, fishlike larval stage during which they breathe through gills which extract oxygen from the water and metamorphose into terrestrial adults equipped with air-breathing lungs. Although some of the modern amphibians are completely aquatic, most can live on land, sometimes even in semiarid regions, as long as they can get enough moisture from their surroundings to prevent dehydration by water loss through their soft skins.

The earliest-known fossils of froglike amphibians stem from the Jurassic period, which later on also saw the emergence of such strange new creatures as the archaeopteryx, the forerunner of modern birds. The frog ancestors of that time already had a well-developed, specialized leg bone structure that equipped them for leaping. Despite the explanation of animal development offered in Darwin's theory of evolution we really have not the slightest idea how and why certain new animal forms appeared seemingly out of nowhere. This is especially true in cases involving complex features such as fully formed feathers, for which no intermediate stages have been found.

Today's living amphibians, a class of animals ranking above the fish and below the reptiles, are divided into three large groups, or orders. The first of these are the caecilians—

Limbless caecilian, most primitive of amphibians, resembles overgrown earthworm.

Four-legged, tailed salamander represents the second of the three amphibian orders.

primitive, secretive amphibians that are rarely seen and hence not well known. The second order includes all the salamanders and newts. The third, the frogs and toads, is the one with which we are here concerned. Their order, the Salientia or "leaping ones," is the largest of the three and is subdivided into 18 families comprising some 250 genera and about 2,500 species. The terms "frog" and "toad," in strict biological usage, are correctly applied only to a single family each. Although the other groups are also variously—and often interchangeably—known as frogs or toads, a qualifying word such as "clawed" or "midwife" is often added. That the lines are not clearly drawn can be seen from the fact that tree frogs are frequently called tree toads, both names being equally correct. When discussing collectively members of different families, biologists can get around the difficulty by grouping them as *anurans,* which comes from the Greek and means the tailless ones.

Since that time so many millions of years ago when the first froglike ancestors leaped to capture insects on the wing, frogs and toads have not only survived but, in fact, spread over the entire globe and adapted to almost every kind of environment and habitat despite their moisture-requiring skin. Only the completely waterless desert areas and the regions of permanent freezing cold are without any amphibian life whatever. Nor can amphibians live in the ocean. Salt water is almost immediately fatal to practically all of them, although a very few exceptions have built up enough immunity to salt water to make their home in brackish pools.

In order to overcome a variety of environmental obstacles, frogs and toads have availed themselves of various types of anatomical modifications and behavior patterns that aid them in survival. Thus we find them hidden away in moisture-conserving burrows in the arid regions of central Australia and Africa; adapting the length of their metamorphosis to the short summers of the very cold regions of Alaska and northern Sweden; and utilizing the seepage of springs in the cracks and crevices of the windswept slopes of the Andean and Himalayan mountains. The greatest number and variety, however, are found in the tropical and subtropical regions. There abound the giants as well as the dwarfs, the completely arboreal species, the gaudily colored frogs whose brilliant color patterns make them look more like artifacts than living beings.

Despite the great differences in size, shape, and body proportions, all frogs and toads share certain essential anatomical features as well as the necessity of going through a metamorphosis—usually in some body of water—from tailed, legless, fishlike larva to tailless, four-legged adult.

When resting, the typical salientian sits in a crouching position, its anterior body supported by short front legs. The long hind legs, whose special structure equips the animals for leaping or hopping, are folded so that the knee joint comes to rest above the toes. This is made possible by an extremely flexible ankle joint and a very long hind foot, which combine to give the animal the leverage needed to take off in a jump from a sitting position.

The eyes, which often have beautiful gold-colored irises, are usually large and prominent and are located so that the frog has a wide range of vision. Moving objects, prey as well as enemy, can be perceived coming from almost all directions; it is therefore not easy to creep up to a frog from behind. Their vision is good, and the ability to see a wide range of colors is evidently well developed.

Most frogs and toads have voices and like to use them. Millions of years before birds sang on our planet, choruses of frogs must have made music in the swamps and bogs of that strange world so long ago. Males are the main, and in some species the only musicians. The voices of the females are heard much more rarely. Many salientians have inflatable vocal sacs, which during their "songs" are visible either as a single pouch below the throat or as a pair of balloon-like bubbles protruding from the sides of the head near the armpits. The

Frogs with two different types of external vocal pouches.

A frog with a largely internal vocal pouch.

ears, or tympani, are membrane disks located just below and behind the eyes; there is no external ear structure.

The mouths of the majority of frogs are wide and can accommodate astonishingly large items of food that have to be swallowed whole, for the teeth, where they exist, are usually very small and made only for holding prey, not for biting and chewing. Most frogs are aided in capturing their prey by the use of a flexible tongue attached at the front of the lower jaw. This tongue can be shot out with great speed to reach, encircle, and draw back into the mouth any insect or other small creature that ventures too close. Too fast to be visible to the unaided human eye, the flick of the tongue can be caught by high-speed cameras, and the films, run in slow motion, have given us exact knowledge of how the tongue mechanism works. One of the more fascinating details revealed by such films was the fact that the frog's eyes retract as the tongue is shot out. This means that he cannot see his target during the leap and can capture it only because he has correctly gauged the distance in advance.

The sense of smell is poorly developed in most adult anurans; the sense of taste, however, seems to be keen,

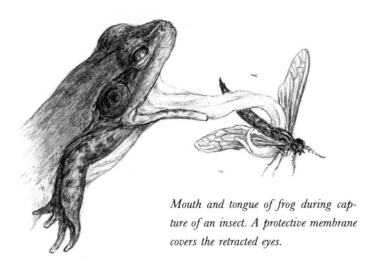

Mouth and tongue of frog during capture of an insect. A protective membrane covers the retracted eyes.

judging from the number of taste buds found in the mouth. Although the ability to taste a worm or a slug may seem somewhat superfluous to us, the taste buds evidently permit the frog to quickly eject noxious, evil-tasting insects.

The sense of touch is well developed in all members, and their primary organ of the tactile sense is the skin, in which many free nerve endings are found. A frog's skin serves it not only by absorbing the necessary moisture from its surroundings—no amphibian ever *drinks* water—but also by lubricating its body with the help of special glands. Moreover, the frog's skin informs it of a variety of environmental conditions ranging from changes in humidity to possible dangers lurking in the vicinity. Thus even the feather-light touch of a leaf bending in the wind will send a frog leaping for safety.

In addition to the mucous skin glands that lubricate the frog's body surface, there are other, granular glands which secrete more or less poisonous, acrid substances. In their milder forms, these secretions only irritate the membranes of the mouth and eyes of would-be predators, but the most potent are capable of paralyzing and even killing animals as large as fully grown dogs or wolves. Many anurans with especially toxic secretions have brilliant colors in combinations believed by some experts to be "warning patterns."

The typical frog or toad begins its life when the female lays her soft, jelly-covered eggs into the water of a pool or pond

Eggs of a frog (left) and a toad.

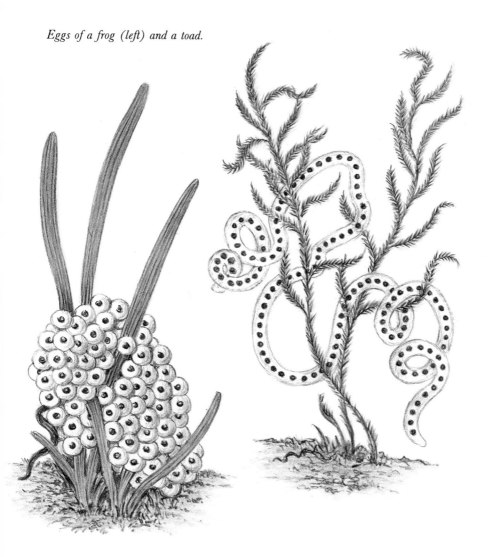

or near the banks of a stream. Depending on the species, they may be deposited singly, in clumps, or in strings, but usually in considerable numbers. The male promptly fertilizes them, and then both parents leave. After a varying period of time, tiny fishlike tadpoles hatch from these eggs and begin searching for the microscopic plants that make up their diet. Most frog larvae are vegetarians, although they may eat some dead animal matter. Their small mouths are equipped with horny, rasplike rims with which they scrape algae and submerged plants. Unlike the adults, the larvae usually have a very good sense of smell.

As the tadpole grows, it also changes. First, tiny stumps appear on both sides of the body at the base of the tail; these stumps gradually develop into long, muscular hind legs. Later, this process is repeated with the front legs, so that the tadpole now begins to resemble a long-tailed frog. During the last stage of metamorphosis, internal changes take place: the long intestine of the plant-eater is replaced by the shorter intestinal tract of the carnivore; gills are replaced by lungs; mouth and eyes change and become larger, until finally a small frog, with a fast-shrinking tail still adhering to its body, climbs onto a large leaf or floating piece of wood or leaves the water altogether for dry land. Within days, the rest of the tail has been absorbed, and a perfect froglet or toadlet joins the ranks of other adult anurans.

The length of the metamorphosis differs greatly with the species and is frequently determined by such external factors as climate, water conditions, and food sources. Thus complete metamorphosis may take as little as ten or twelve days, or as much as a full year. Usually, but not always, the large species

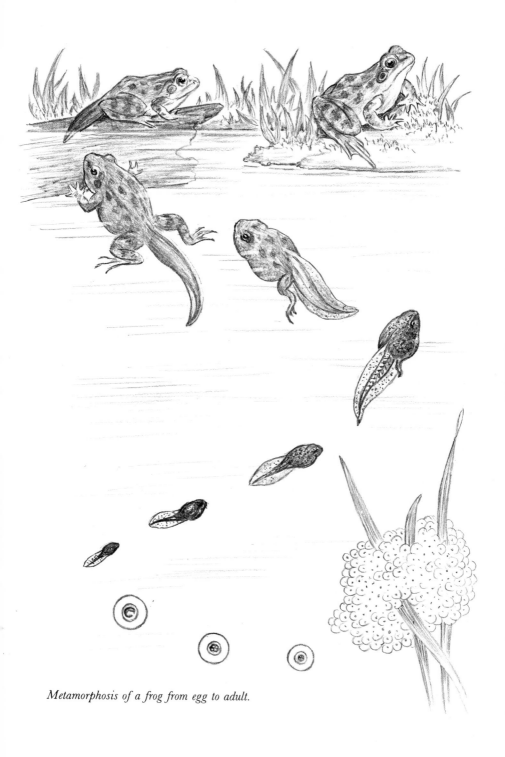

Metamorphosis of a frog from egg to adult.

need a much longer time for development.

From the preceding description of the larval development, it may sound like an easy procedure; actually, however,
the larval stages are the most dangerous for frogs and toads, a
high-risk period fraught with hazards. In their underwater
jungle, the tadpoles are exposed to attack not only by fish and
turtles but also by large, rapacious aquatic insects such as
dragonfly and water beetle larvae. Although these insects
sometimes attack adult frogs, they take an especially heavy toll
of the rather slow-moving and helpless tadpoles. It is easy to
understand why most amphibians have to produce such a

*Larva of a giant water beetle
attacking a tadpole.*

large number of eggs; otherwise there would not be enough surviving offspring in each generation. Those species with relatively few eggs take special measures to increase the survival chances of their progeny, as we shall see in a later chapter.

Even as adults, the anurans are extremely vulnerable; as a group, frogs and toads probably have more enemies than any other animal order. Possessing neither claws nor teeth for self-defense, they are hunted by a variety of predators, ranging from larger relatives to birds and mammals. However, several compensating factors aid them in their struggle for survival. One of the most important is the aforementioned ability to secrete acrid and toxic substances. Equally important is their ability to find good hiding places and to change their color to blend in with whatever background they have selected. Some species are veritable color-change artists, capable of adapting their coloring and pattern to that of the surface they are resting on to an almost incredible degree. Such frogs and toads come close to having that mythical "cloak of invisibility" that plays so great a part in many old legends and fairy tales, for even sharp-eyed enemies will pass right by without spotting them as long as they remain motionless.

The color changes are effected through special pigment cells called chromatophores. Most important are those containing dark brown or black melanin; others may be filled with red or yellow pigment as well as crystalline light reflector granules. Practically no blue pigment is found in the animal world; blue is usually "structural"—meaning that it is created through light dispersal and reflection.

When the pigment granules are aggregated in the center

of the star- or blossom-shaped chromatophores, the animal is light-colored. However, as the granules are dispersed throughout each cell, the color darkens and intensifies.

Tests with frogs have proved that the chief stimuli for color changes in amphibians are visual. Perceiving the colors and patterns of its background with its marvelous eyes, the frog proceeds to adapt its own color to that of its surroundings. Light sensors in the skin also play a role, as do various environmental factors such as temperature and humidity. Many frogs are sensitive to the texture of the surface they are resting on and may change color according to whether the background is rough or smooth.

Chromatophores in various stages of dispersal.

Emotional factors such as fear or excitement also may bring about marked color changes; many frogs and toads pale when frightened, but some, such as the clawed frog of Africa, tend to turn dark when excited or disturbed.

By and large, the anurans' ability to adapt their color to that of their surroundings affords them a considerable degree of protection against their numerous enemies.

Dark pigment is aggregated in center of melanophores; the animal looks green.

Pigment is dispersed throughout melanophores; the animal appears dark.

Mechanism of color changes through pigment dispersal.

Because of such adaptations, and aided by their prolific reproduction, the tailless amphibians have survived the relentless depredations by a host of enemies on land and in the water to become one of the most numerous and widespread groups of vertebrate animals.

2 Primitive Frogs and Toads

The term "primitive" as applied by biologists may be at times confusing to those not versed in scientific terminology. Quite often, there are no visible external features that indicate the difference between the primitive and the more advanced members of any one group, nor is there anything in the primitive groups' behavior that would immediately set them apart from their advanced relatives. In all cases, certain anatomical structures associated with those of common ancestral groups determine the classification. Sometimes the anatomical differences are quite obvious; pythons and boas, for example, have externally visible remnants of legs that tie them more closely to their four-legged serpent ancestors than those snakes that have lost all outside traces of leg structure. The reason why boas and pythons are considered "primitive" snakes is therefore easy for even the nonscientist to understand.

No such easy identification is possible in the case of the tailless amphibians because certain features of the ribs and vertebrae are used by scientists to determine the status of a species within the group. The most primitive family of frogs is very small, consisting of two genera with only four species, one of which, the peculiar tailed frog, is found in the icy mountain streams of the Pacific Northwest. Oddly enough, its only close relatives, three species of small frogs with peculiar habits, live halfway around the world in New Zealand. They prefer high altitudes where there is very little water accumulation because the slopes are steep and the water runs off too quickly. These frogs therefore had to find a way to complete their metamorphosis without the normal free-swimming larval stage common to most anurans. Instead, the tadpole develops inside the egg, which is deposited on moist ground, and finally the froglet, still with a tail attached, hatches directly from the egg. During its first weeks of life the tail is gradually absorbed and the lungs, at first insufficiently developed, become fully functional for air breathing.

The tailed frog of the Pacific Northwest.
Only the male has the distinctive "tail."

The North American species of this family undergoes a normal metamorphosis. The female deposits the eggs in water, attaching them to the lower surfaces of rocks to keep them from being swept away by the swift currents of the mountain streams. The tadpoles manage to survive in the swirling waters by clinging to rocks with a suction organ special to the species at the top of their heads.

Despite the fact that it is descriptive, the popular name "tailed frog" for this amphibian is a misnomer. The taillike appendage of the male—a unique feature found in no other frog or toad species—is actually an organ of copulation, used to introduce the sperm into the female's body during mating.

Another strange family of primitive frogs, with members in South America and Africa, is the group known as the tongueless frogs. As the name indicates, these amphibians are distinguished by the lack of a tongue. In both appearance and habits they are quite peculiar, for not only are they almost completely aquatic, with the physical modifications necessary for such a life, but they also are partly scavengers, eating dead animals as well as live ones. This is a most unusual practice for frogs, most of which will not touch anything that does not move. The large hind feet of the tongueless frogs are heavily webbed. Their front limbs are equipped with long, slender, mobile fingers with which they probe the mud at the bottom of the rivers in which they live, grabbing and eating any small creature—dead or alive—they can find.

The most familiar of the South American species is the so-called Surinam toad, which gained fame when its strange breeding habits were first recorded 150 years ago. In chapter seven, these habits will be described in detail.

The Surinam toad and its close relatives are ungainly-looking creatures with flat bodies, small, beady eyes, and pointed noses. Almost helpless out of water, which they never leave unless forced to do so, they are good swimmers and quite agile as they move about in the water. All the members of this genus *Pipa* live in the equatorial regions of South America, especially in the Guianas and Venezuela.

The African members of the family include the well-known clawed frogs. On the three inner toes, these amphibians have tiny claws whose function has not yet been fully established. The genus *Xenopus* became famous as the first frogs used in tests designed to establish proof of pregnancy in women. It was discovered that the urine of a woman injected into an unfertilized female clawed frog caused it to lay eggs if the woman was pregnant. No reaction occurred in the frog if the woman was not pregnant. Until scientists found out that most other female frogs could be used in pregnancy tests, the laboratory demand for clawed frogs was overwhelming.

Clawed frogs look perhaps a little less like a bizarre caricature of a frog than their close South American relatives. Their bodies are not quite as flat as those of the Surinam toads, their eyes are larger, and they can move around a little better on land. In the water, they are strong and skillful, excellent swimmers and divers.

One of the best known of the clawed frogs is *Xenopus laevis*, known in South Africa as the platanna. It grows to a length of about five inches, and its insatiable appetite is of tremendous importance in that region, since the waters of those parts of Africa teem with the larvae of mosquitoes that transmit malaria and other serious infectious diseases. Tests with

The pipa, or Surinam toad. The heavily webbed feet proclaim the aquatic habits of this species. Star-shaped filament clusters on the tips of its long fingers are sensitive organs of touch.

captive platannas have shown that they devour these insects in record numbers. We can only guess at the value of these frogs in the wild in the prevention of suffering and death from mosquito-borne disease.

Because the rivers in which they live usually dry up during the rainless summer season, the clawed frogs burrow

The African clawed frog, or platanna.

deep into damp soil and remain there "summering" until the rains come with the onset of winter—the counterpart behavior of their relatives in northern latitudes that spend a similar enforced resting period hibernating during the cold winter months. No food is consumed during these months of inactivity; the frogs' metabolism is lowered sufficiently for them to endure the long fast without difficulty, and they gain weight rapidly once the weather permits them to emerge and feed again.

Among the more handsome of the primitive groups are the fire-bellied toads, which have several genera with wide distribution in Africa, Asia, and Europe, but have no representatives in the Western Hemisphere. They are prominently aquatic, although not as much so as the tongueless frogs. Many leave the water for short excursions on land in search of insects, but none of them venture far from the protective depths of the pools or streams in which they live. The distinctive anatomical feature of this family is a disk-shaped tongue that cannot be extended beyond the rim of the mouth.

From above, most fire-bellies look relatively dull and drab, with patterns of dark gray, brownish, and olive hues. All this changes drastically whenever the toad feels threatened. Rearing up so that its underside is exposed, it displays a vivid pattern of black and bright yellow or fiery orange spots and blotches—a startling and unexpected contrast to its topside. As long as the toad believes the danger exists, it maintains this rigidly erect display position, designed to convince a predator that so brilliantly colored a creature cannot possibly be good to eat and should be left alone. Nor is the warning given in vain to an experienced predator. The skin secretions of these

European fire-bellied toad.

small toads are very caustic and poisonous, thus making their capture an unpleasant and painful surprise that is not easily forgotten.

Most fire-bellies average about two inches; even the largest species does not exceed a length of three inches. Their voices are rather weak but may be quite musical and bell-like. Europe has both a northern and a southern species; Asia has several, including a handsome toad that is bright green and black above, orange and black below. This species lives in parts of China, Manchuria, and Korea; practically nothing is known about its habits.

The most famous members of the family are the two insignificant-looking and drab-colored small toads of the genus *Alytes*, the midwife toads of Europe. The better-known of the two species is *Alytes obstetricans*, whose unique breeding behavior, described in a later chapter, made it the object of special attention by naturalists in the early part of the last century. Much later this toad became the center of a scientific argument about certain questions of evolutionary development.

Also classed among the more primitive families of Salientia is the group known as spadefoot toads. In contrast to the preceding family, which is limited to the Eastern Hemisphere, several species of spadefoots are found in North America. Others occur in Europe, Africa, and Asia, and are generally chunky, squat frogs with a horny, crescent-shaped "spade" at the side of the foot which explains their popular name. The spade is a useful tool, enabling these toads to dig themselves quickly into loose or sandy soil with an ease and efficiency that are quite astonishing. This ability comes in handy for those species living in regions so arid that they have to remain in underground burrows for weeks at a time to escape the dehydrating effect of the intense dry heat above ground. For such species as, for instance, Hurter's and Couch's spadefoot, both of the American southwest, access to water suitable for breeding is the all-important problem, for the larvae of these toads have a normal free-swimming stage. In order to overcome this difficulty, these spadefoots have adapted to breeding whenever conditions are favorable—that is, whenever a rainfall has filled the temporary pools in their semiarid habitats. At these pools, spadefoots from all over aggregate in numbers to deposit and fertilize their eggs.

All this, however, would not be enough by itself to insure the species' survival unless the development of the larvae could be speeded up enough for them to keep pace with the rate of evaporation of the temporary pools. Accordingly, the tadpoles of Hurter's spadefoot hatch from the eggs after only two days and may complete their metamorphosis within twelve days if the food sources are adequate; otherwise, development is much slower. If the larvae die because the pool dries out before they attain adulthood, their remains make nourishing food for next rainy season's crop of tadpoles, which then can complete their metamorphosis much more quickly. Thus even dead tadpoles help to insure the continued survival of their kind.

Other members of the family—such as the common spadefoot of eastern North America—never lack enough permanent bodies of water suitable for breeding and thus have a much longer, normal larval development.

The European spadefoot toad is found all over that continent and also in Asia Minor. In Germany it is known as *Knoblauchkroete*, meaning garlic toad, because its skin secretion, produced especially when it is frightened or handled roughly, has a garlic-like odor. Many toads give off distinctive odors that are not always unpleasant, at least to human noses. One toad, for instance, smells like vanilla. Captive garlic toads that are treated gently soon stop secreting the strong-smelling exudation.

North American spadefoot toad.

Some other spadefoots in Asia have a very peculiar appearance; thus the Asiatic horned frog, which despite its name is a spadefoot toad, has hornlike skin projections over the eyes and at the tip of its snout. Together with its "cat's eyes"—vertical pupils that proclaim the nocturnal animal—these projections give this toad a somewhat sinister expression, which may not be altogether misleading since this species is thought to be cannibalistic.

With the spadefoot toads, the list of frog families considered to be more primitive than the rest is complete. We will now turn our attention to the three large groups—the toads, the tree frogs, and the true frogs—that include the best-known species in the temperate regions of the world.

3 Toads

True toads are found in almost every part of the world, tropical as well as temperate, that can sustain amphibian life, with the exception only of the Australasian region and Madagascar. South America, mainland Asia, and Africa average roughly the same number of species, between sixty-five and seventy-five, of the type genus *Bufo*. (A type genus is the group after which the family is named.) North America has about two dozen if we include Central America, whereas Europe runs way behind with only three.

Almost everyone who has a garden is familiar with one or more species of toads, although identification of any particular species may at times be quite difficult. This is especially true because certain species may have different races, or subspecies, that vary considerably in size and color. In eastern North America, the American toad and Fowler's toad are common, widespread, and abundant; farther west, such species as the Great Plains toad, the Rocky Mountain toad, and others take their place.

Fowler's toad calling.

Although the individual species may not be readily identifiable except by an expert, toads are easy to recognize as members of their group. They have squat, chunky bodies, shorter hind legs than frogs, and usually very warty skins. The skin protuberances which superstition blames for producing warts on the skin of a person who touches a toad have, of course, no relationship to real warts, which are caused by a virus. However, toads do secrete a poisonous substance from the two prominent parotoid glands located behind the eyes and just above the tympani. The secretions of the individual species may vary considerably in the degree of toxicity, but even those with relatively low toxicity cause a burning sensation on the mucous membranes of the mouth and eyes. This helps protect toads against a number of enemies sensitive to the poison. How well it works can be seen from the reactions of such predators as foxes, wolves, or coyotes that have once tried to eat a toad and are later confronted with these

46

amphibians. Striking proof of the potency of at least some toads' poison was reported by Doris M. Cochran, Curator of Reptiles and Amphibians at the Smithsonian Institution, in her book on living amphibians of the world. According to a report cited by her, a police dog made the mistake of taking a large Colorado toad in its mouth. A short while later, the dog was dead from the effects of the poison.

Such examples do not mean that humans handling toads need be afraid of their secretions. The only precaution they should observe—and a good one to observe after handling *any* animal—is to thoroughly wash their hands afterward and to never bring their unwashed hands in contact with eyes and mouth.

Toad poison is a complex substance made up of various proteins. In ancient China, physicians used it in the treatment of heart ailments. Modern chemical analysis reveals that phrynin, one of the poison's components, is a digitalis-like substance. Since digitalis is widely used in the treatment of heart conditions today, modern research has confirmed the astuteness of the old Chinese physicians.

Because of their life-style, toads are generally much more

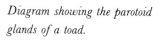

Diagram showing the parotoid glands of a toad.

beneficial to man than frogs. The latter are usually more or less restricted to areas bordering on water and are found mainly in the vicinity of ponds and pools and along riverbanks. Toads, on the other hand, are not so restricted and often wander far from the water, preferring to take up their abodes in gardens and fields and among other cultivated vegetation, where they consume a tremendous number of harmful insects and other plant-eating pests such as slugs. The destructive larvae of many beetles—the infamous cutworms and wireworms, for instance—as well as a host of others fall prey to the insatiable appetite of the gardeners' and farmers' unassuming but faithful amphibious friends.

General recognition of the toad's usefulness has been slow. A century ago, the German naturalist Alfred Brehm scolded continental Europeans for letting their superstitions influence them in their behavior toward toads. "Those who indulge, through blind prejudice, in the killing of these beneficial creatures," he wrote, "thereby furnish proof only of their own ignorance and brutishness. The English gardeners have learned long ago what great benefits they derive from the insatiable appetite of these animals for harmful plant eaters such as slugs and insect larvae, and at this writing are buying toads by the dozen to let them work in their gardens." Crops such as lettuce, which are especially exposed to damage by slugs in many regions, can be protected efficiently, inexpensively, and without harming the environment, by maintaining a sufficiently large population of toads.

What makes these amphibians so valuable is the fact that they do not wander far from "home" once they have established themselves in a given territory. This affinity of

48

The formidable Colorado toad.

toads for their favorite home grounds is bolstered by a keen homing instinct that permits them to return unerringly to their chosen breeding territories even from a considerable distance. Because of the toad's longevity, the owner of a garden in which a toad has taken up residence and feels comfortable can count upon having his amphibian friend as a permanent resident for many years to come. The record may be held by an English toad, reported to have lived for thirty-six years under the front steps of a house, becoming so tame that it would come out to have its back scratched and to accept food offered by the inhabitants of the house.

A full-grown marine, or giant, toad.

People who raise certain crops commercially have availed themselves of the toads' good offices. Sugar planters expecting immense benefits at minimum expense to themselves have imported the large toad *Bufo marinus* into every country where sugarcane is grown commercially, to protect their crops against damage caused by the sugarcane beetle. This small beetle, which belongs to the scarab family, is extremely destructive to sugarcane. But with the toads policing the plantations the damage is kept to a minimum. The marine toad, also called the giant toad, whose native habitat includes most of South and Central America and which has entered the most southwestern parts of the United States, is now also well established in places such as Hawaii, Haiti, Puerto Rico, Guam, and the Solomon Islands, where it helps protect crops valued at several billion dollars per year.

Most toads are very prolific, laying great numbers of eggs each breeding season, and some of them are indeed the champion egg layers among the amphibians. The marine toad may produce as many as thirty-five thousand eggs in a single year, and the common southern toad of the southern United States, although much smaller, comes close to that record number with twenty-eight thousand eggs. Tadpoles of the latter species complete their metamorphosis within approximately four weeks. Although many by that time have been eaten by predators, enough tiny toadlets attain adulthood to emerge from their native pond in huge numbers, thereby explaining the popular belief that it may "rain frogs" at certain times. Occasionally, of course, there are good grounds for that belief, for a hurricane may sweep up water from ponds with small fish, frogs, and toads in it and later deposit this "rain" of living animals at some other point in its path. However, when the tiny toads are all of the same size, it must be assumed that they are the result of a mass emergence of newly metamorphosed young.

Of the baby toads, very few survive to grow to maturity, for despite their distasteful glandular secretions, many animals, including larger members of their own tribe, do not hesitate to eat them. At least one kind of nonpoisonous North American snake, the hognose, lives almost exclusively on toads.

Of the three European species, the most familiar and widespread is the common toad, *Bufo bufo*, the prototype of the family. It occurs not only over practically all of Europe, with the exception of the northernmost parts, but also in Central

The European common toad.

The widely distributed green toad of Europe and Asia.

Asia. A fair-sized animal of between four and five inches when fully grown, its coloring is a dull dark brown which often shades into olive. In Germany, it is called *Erdkroete,* "earth toad," as much for its rather drab coloring as for its habit of hiding in burrows.

Then there is the green, or variable, toad *Bufo viridis,* which normally displays green spots on a grayish background. The European range of this toad is limited to the central and southern parts. It does, however, occur on the northeast coast of Africa as well as in Central Africa, and has the distinction of being the only member of the family that has been found at an altitude of fifteen thousand feet in the Himalayan Mountains. As its original scientific name *Bufo variabilis* indicates, the green toad is noted for its ability to change color. Although all anurans possess this ability in varying degrees, it is more pronounced in the green toad than in most of its close relatives. Changes in environmental factors such as temperature and humidity can within a short time turn a vividly

53

green-spotted toad into a pasty gray animal.

The third and last of the European species is the natterjack toad, whose very short hind limbs force it to run somewhat like a mouse instead of hopping along like others of its kind. More colorful than the common toad, it is usually olive green above, with a distinctive light dorsal stripe and reddish warts that often have a light spot in the center.

Some of the most common North American toads have already been mentioned. Other North American species include the western toad and the oak toad. The western toad, also often called the northern toad, is found in much of the Pacific coastal regions and ranges northward to southern Alaska. A pretty little toad, handsomely patterned, is the oak toad of the southern United States. Only a little over an inch long, it has a conspicuous light line running down the center of the back which serves as a good identifying mark. Despite its

An American toad,
a common eastern species.

The oak toad, smallest of the American species.

name, the oak toad prefers to live in the pine woods of its range.

Most people are interested in extremes of size; the giants and the dwarfs of any group are always fascinating. The real dwarfs among the salientians are not found in the toad family, but some of the giants are. All of them occur in Central and South America and some extend slightly into the southwestern United States. We have already mentioned the marine toad, often also called the giant toad, which ranges over much of South and Central America. The length of this toad has been recorded at just over nine inches, although individuals of that size are rare. Another giant is the very handsome Blomberg's toad, which also attains a length of between nine and ten inches. Improbable as it may seem that such a Goliath could be overlooked for so long, Blomberg's toad was not discovered until about twenty years ago. It lives in the rain-drenched foothills of the Cordillera Mountains of Colombia. And then there is the rococo toad, *Bufo paracnemis,* possibly the largest of them all at a recorded length of ten

Blomberg's toad, a recent discovery.

inches. Found in Brazil and Bolivia, this giant has poison glands along the calves of its legs in addition to its large parotoid glands. It is likely that the toxic qualities of its secretions are formidable and afford the animal excellent protection. Its habits are mainly nocturnal, and it hardly ever seems to feed by day; the preferred food appears to be very similar to that of other toads, consisting mainly of slugs, isopods, and the larger insect larvae.

Africa has a great many toads of different genera living in a variety of habitats. The one with the greatest range is probably the leopard toad, *Bufo regularis,* which is found from Arabia all the way south to the Cape. It is interesting to note that, although several dozen different toads occur in Africa, not a single species lives in Madagascar, which is separated from the African mainland by a relatively narrow stretch of water.

Africa may not be able to match South America's record for giant toads, but it does harbor one of the world's smallest species, the tiny Rose's toad, which lives on mountainous slopes in South Africa. Only about an inch long, the female still manages to lay some seven thousand eggs during each breeding season.

A unique toad genus about which we shall hear more in a later chapter is *Nectophrynoides.* Its two species are restricted to Africa, whereas the closely related genus *Nectophryne* is represented by members both in Africa and in southern Asia. The second group is most unusual because of its ability to climb trees, which normally is not included among the habits of toads. The diet of the *Nectophryne* species consists largely of ants. At the other end of the scale are the aquatic toads of the

The aquatic "false" toad of Malaysia.

genus *Pseudobufo* of Malaysia. They spend most of their life in the water, have heavily webbed feet, and have nostrils so located that they protrude out of the water as the toads float near the surface.

The toad considered by many to be the most beautiful of the entire group is also an Asian species, *Bufo melanostictus,* the black-spined toad of southeastern Asia. Normally brown and tan and covered with small black-tipped tubercles, the male may display rose-colored spots during breeding time.

Although amphibian intelligence generally is of a relatively low level, toads are considered to be somewhat more intelligent than frogs. Related to their greater intelligence is their greater curiosity. Most tame quite easily, learning to come out of hiding when food is offered to them and to take it from their owners' fingers without hesitation. Some become so tame that they actually like to be handled, especially if their backs are scratched gently, which most seem to enjoy very much.

Future research and observation may reveal many additional interesting aspects of their behavior. In any case, despite their homely appearance, toads should be appreciated for the valuable services they render, and should be afforded every possible protection as important members of nature's system of checks and balances on which the health of our natural environment is based.

4 Tree Frogs

Besides being one of the largest families within the order of the Salientia, tree frogs are also one of the most colorful. In addition, their acrobatic talents make them amusing as well as interesting to watch—they have been called the clowns and high-wire artists of the amphibian world.

Most tree frogs are small, averaging a body length of less than two inches, with many species attaining only half that size. The giant of the clan does not exceed a length of six inches, just slightly more than half the size of some of the giant toads and true frogs, and the family has a great number of "dwarfs" measuring one inch or less. The requirements of an arboreal existence are of course much more easily fulfilled by small, lightweight creatures.

What the tree frogs lack in size, they more than make up for by their other qualities. Not only do many of them have bright and attractive colors; they are also the champion color-change artists among amphibians. The list of their talents would not be complete without mentioning the fact

North American spring peeper calling.

that many of them are excellent vocalists. A number of arboreal frogs are renowned for their loud, clear, musical calls and the enthusiasm with which they perform their concerts on warm spring and summer nights, especially during the breeding season.

Tree frogs are found in practically every part of the world where toads are found, as well as in Australia, which has no native toads. The almost five hundred species of tree frogs have managed to adapt to a number of different habitats and climates, ranging from tropical jungles to the Canadian woods, and from sea level to altitudes of up to fifteen thousand feet. The tropical regions have of course the greatest variety and number of species.

Much more lightly built than toads, tree frogs have pads, or disks, on their fingers and toes that act like suction cups, thereby permitting the frogs to cling even to smooth, slippery surfaces such as leaves. Their long slender legs give them the power for graceful leaps, during which their arms and legs are spread wide on the same plane as their bodies in order to increase the supporting surface.

The majority of tree frogs have normal breeding habits. Their eggs are deposited in water, and they go through a free-swimming larval stage. A few, however, are distinguished by deviations from the norm that make their breeding behavior especially interesting, as will be discussed in chapter seven.

In North America, the most common tree frogs, as well as the ones with the widest range, are the spring peeper and the gray, or variable, tree frog. They are found over the entire eastern half of the United States and parts of southern Canada. The spring peeper ranges somewhat farther north than its larger cousin—which is not really large either, seeing that it attains the hardly impressive length of two inches. In comparison to the spring peeper, however, which averages just about an inch, the gray is a hefty individual.

Despite its small size, the spring peeper has an astonishingly loud, clear voice, and enjoys using it. Its high, piping whistles have great carrying power and can be heard as far away as a mile. If uttered by a large chorus of these frogs, the calls sound somewhat like sleigh bells.

In the south, spring peepers breed from November to March; in the northeast they begin their courtship music early in the spring, usually after the first warm rain. To many people in that region, spring would not be truly spring without the musical contributions of these tiny frogs. In view of that, it is surprising that relatively few people ever see a spring peeper, although so many know them from their calls. The fact is that the tiny musicians are difficult to spot because their brownish or greenish coloring blends perfectly into the background of the pond they have selected for breeding. The footsteps of a person approaching the pond will immediately still all the voices in that particular choral group. If the intruder remains motionless for a few minutes, the peepers will begin again, and then it should be possible to spot some of the small creatures, each usually with a distinctive cross mark on its back. In order to produce so loud a call, the vocal sac of the spring peeper has to be inflated until it becomes a balloon that appears out of all proportion to the size of the frog.

The gray tree frog, which shares most of the spring

Gray, or variable, tree frog in gray-green phase.

Gray tree frog in brown color phase.

peeper's range, and the similar but smaller bird-voiced tree frog are found in swampy woodland areas. They usually spend most of their lives in trees and shrubs and rarely come down except during the breeding season. The normal pattern of the gray tree frog looks very much like the lichens on old trees in its habitat, but it can change its color to solid green or brown or to a variety of patterns as the situation demands. Because this frog is capable of keeping perfectly still for prolonged periods, its color camouflage is very effective in concealing it from the eyes of its enemies.

The tiny chorus and cricket frogs are about the size of the

spring peeper and are also endowed with loud voices that are not, however, as musical. Much of their range coincides with that of the spring peeper, and in some regions there may be a mixed chorus, coming from a single pond, in which the different calls can be clearly identified. Cricket frogs are champion jumpers but lack the adhesive disks of other tree frogs and can therefore climb only with difficulty.

Considering their small size, their metamorphosis is very long, taking anything from fifty to ninety days depending upon weather conditions. Like most others of their kind, the newly emerged cricket froglets, less than one-half inch long, are beset by a host of enemies that include their larger relatives as well as herons, grackles, turtles, and snakes.

Chorus frogs, of which the ornate chorus frog is one of the prettiest representatives, have toe disks and are often found in

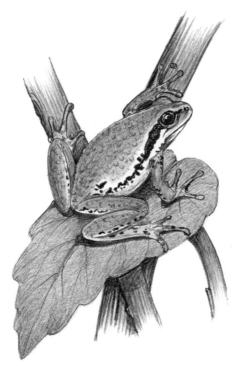

North American Pacific tree frog.

Bird-voiced tree frog.

Green tree frog.

Ornate chorus frog.

Three small species of American tree frogs.

low shrubs and reeds near the edge of a pond or in a swamp. There are more than a dozen species of chorus frogs in North America, and their range extends from southern Canada through the eastern and central United States and into Mexico.

The southern regions of the United States are inhabited by a number of other tree frogs including the barking tree frog, whose call sounds somewhat like the yapping of a small dog; the pine woods and squirrel tree frogs; and the green tree frog, probably the handsomest of them all. Restricted to small portions of the extreme south and southwest are such essentially Central American species as the Cuban and Mexican tree frogs.

In the west, the most common and widespread species is the Pacific tree frog, which occurs along the coastal regions from Canada to Mexico. The canyon tree frog has adapted to conditions in semiarid regions of the southwest and lives in tree-lined canyons in New Mexico, Arizona, and California. It never strays very far from mountain streams, and its larvae have a normal free-swimming stage.

Some of the outstanding tree frogs of Central and South America include the Cuban tree frog, most common in Cuba and the Bahamas, where it likes to make its home in epiphytic plants. This type of plant, which includes most tropical orchids and many others, lives on the branches of trees. It is not a parasite but gets its nourishment from the air, the water, and the little bit of organic matter that accumulates in the crevices of its host tree's bark.

The Cuban tree frog has very large toe disks and a rough warty skin. It attains the considerable length of five inches.

Another interesting and equally large South American member of the family is the smith frog of Brazil, whose unusual breeding habits will be discussed later. The name of this species was inspired by its peculiar call, which sounds somewhat like beating on tin pans.

Among the strangest members of the clan are the bony-headed tree frogs of the Central and South American tropics. The skulls of these frogs are thickened into bony casques and fused to the skin. Rarely seen because of their nocturnal habits, most of these frogs have hoarse, unmusical voices. During the day they hide in clusters of epiphytic plants such as orchids, where their coloring tends to camouflage them as long as they do not move.

Europe has only one common species of tree frog, which occurs throughout that continent with the exception only of the far northern parts and Great Britain. A close relative, the Mediterranean tree frog, is limited to the coastal regions and the islands of the Mediterranean Sea.

Common European tree frog.

In the manner of its clan, the European tree frog can change its color considerably. Variations in atmospheric conditions may induce a bright green individual to pale to a pasty buff or darken to a deep green. An abnormally dark-colored frog does not always, however, represent a color-change phase; it may be a *melano*—the opposite of an albino—in which the yellow pigment is lacking, whereas the dark melanin and the cells that reflect blue light are present. Such frogs usually display a shade of blue ranging from turquoise to blue gray; melanos occur among all types of frogs.

The European tree frog is approximately the same size and coloring as its North American cousin of the same name but is much more widely known in the countries where it occurs than any American tree frog in its home territory. Traditionally, the European species was a favorite pet. Many children who grew up in Europe felt disadvantaged unless they had their own "tame" tree frog, usually sold by pet shops complete with a small terrarium equipped with a tiny ladder. The cost was negligible, the upkeep inexpensive and easy, and

A normally colored tree frog and a blue melano—*an individual without yellow pigment.*

the proud owner could predict the weather, announcing to his or her family that the coming day would be fine (the frog was sitting on the top rung of the ladder and was quiet) or rainy (the frog stayed at the bottom and was croaking). Although they are far from being infallible weather prophets, apart from the fact that females do not croak, the behavior of these frogs is to a large extent dictated by atmospheric conditions and often does foretell changes in the weather. By and large, and considering the frequent errors made by our own sophisticated weather stations, the performance of the little forecasters must be rated as from fair to good.

Asia has its own generous quota of tree frogs, of which the green tree frog—the third species with the identical popular name—is a good example. This rather secretive nocturnal species breeds in the rice paddies, ponds, and stagnant pools of western China. It is very good at concealing itself among clumps of bamboo or other vegetation, from which its voice may be heard without the owner ever being seen.

Australia and the East Indian region harbor some seventy species of tree frogs; many of these are insufficiently known, with little or no recorded information about their life-styles and habits.

Two handsome and easily tamed Australian hylids—the scientific name of the tree frog family is Hylidae—are the golden tree frog and White's tree frog. The former was named for the gold-colored stripe along each side, though its back is green. White's tree frog is all green, with a smooth shiny skin that looks almost artificial. This frog seems to like the proximity of human beings. It is said to come of its own volition to porches and houses on summer evenings and, if captured, tames quickly and accepts insects from its owner's fingers without hesitation.

Africa has many fewer tree frogs than either tropical America or Asia, and very little is known about their life histories. A group of primarily African frogs formerly classed with the tree frogs, but since placed in the separate family Rhacophoridae, includes some extremely interesting, brilliantly colored species that will be dealt with in chapter seven.

Although the type genus *Hyla* accounts for the majority of tree frogs, there are a number of smaller genera with interesting members, for example those of *Phyllomedusa*, nocturnal, "cat-eyed," and often very handsomely patterned frogs of South America.

Although tree frogs have no giants among their ranks, since both large size and weight would work to the disadvantage of arboreal species, they do have a great number of very small members. The tiniest of all the known tree frogs, and one

*A cat-eyed tree frog
of the genus* Phyllomedusa.

Cricket frog and little grass frog, both shown life size.

of the smallest of the entire order, is the little grass frog of southern North America. It averages five-eighths of an inch; the largest individual ever recorded was just under three-quarters of an inch long. This charming little creature ranges from southeastern Virginia to Florida and Alabama, where it lives especially in cypress swamps. It always stays relatively close to the ground, climbing around in low vegetation along the banks of ponds, from where its shrill, tinkling call can be heard. Newly metamorphosed little grass froglets (the "little" is part of the common name of this species) are less than a quarter of an inch long.

Attractive colors, musical voices, acrobatic talents, elfin proportions—one or more of these attributes can be found in almost any species of tree frog. If we add to that their useful feeding habits, it is easy to understand why so many people feel that tree frogs are probably the most appealing and engaging group of amphibians.

5 True Frogs

So many species in the preceding chapter look so much like the popular concept of a "true" frog, whatever that is supposed to be, that most people find themselves understandably confused about the use of the term. However, certain anatomical features have convinced scientists to apply that term only to the genus *Rana* and related genera. The family Ranidae, whose members include the most familiar species, such as the bull, leopard, and grass frogs, are found on all continents, although the southern parts of both South America and Australia have no native representatives, and neither has New Zealand.

The typical frog has a streamlined, bullet-shaped, more or less smooth-skinned body; long, muscular legs with toes joined by webs; and no adhesive pads on toes and fingers. The head is pointed, the eardrums and the protruding eyes are large.

The type genus *Rana*, a predominantly Old World group, is nevertheless the only genus represented in North America,

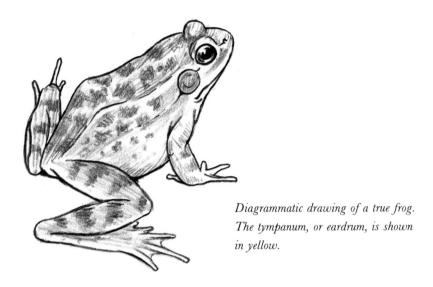

Diagrammatic drawing of a true frog. The tympanum, or eardrum, is shown in yellow.

which harbors about a dozen species. Largest and most famous is the bullfrog, which averages a length of five inches, but in exceptional cases may grow to about eight inches long. This is the frog whose large, fleshy hind legs are served as delicacies in North American restaurants. Because these frogs need a long time to attain maturity—metamorphosis takes a full year, and the young bullfrog is not fully mature for another five years—hunting them for commercial purposes quickly depletes the population of specimens large enough to warrant capture.

The bullfrog's name has nothing to do with its size. Instead, as in the case of many other frogs, it refers to its loud, resonant voice, likened by some to the bellow of a bull. A large concentration of bullfrogs sounding off together during the night can understandably drive any unfortunate human neighbor to distraction, for they display the same unflagging enthusiasm in their choral performances as many of their smaller relatives. One European traveler, returning home

*North American bullfrog
floating among water plants.*

from a visit to the south of the United States, reported that he had been unable to sleep for three consecutive nights because of the nocturnal concerts.

The natural range of the bullfrog has been greatly extended since its introduction into the western parts of the United States. Originally, it was found only east of the Rockies.

Because of their large size, adult bullfrogs can swallow relatively large prey and are not satisfied with an all-insect diet. They will eat almost anything they can overpower, including smaller frogs, very young water birds, fish, and young turtles, whose shells are dissolved by the frog's strong digestive juices. Bullfrogs are frequently accused of drowning and eating ducklings. Although this may happen occasionally, only very large individuals could manage to swallow anything as big as a duckling. We must remember that a frog has no

The common green frog.

The pickerel frog.

teeth for biting and chewing, so that every food item must be swallowed whole, and although its mouth is large, it does not have the hinged jaw that permits a snake to swallow items several times the circumference of its own body.

In most instances where ducklings are pulled under water and drowned by something lurking beneath the surface, the culprit is not a bullfrog but a large snapping turtle, which can tear even large prey to pieces with its razor-sharp beak. Since much of the bullfrog's natural range coincides with that of the snapping turtle, the two often share the same habitat—which means that the frogs also have to be on constant alert against these predators.

Other common and familiar North American frogs include the green frog, widespread throughout the east, and the attractively patterned leopard and pickerel frogs. The

79

leopard frog has the greater range, being found throughout the entire United States and large parts of Canada with the exception only of the Pacific regions. The pickerel frog is an eastern species and one of the handsomest of all North American frogs. It has a distinctive pattern of squarish dark brown spots on a metallic bronze or gold-colored background. It is also the one with the most poisonous skin secretions. Unless these secretions come into contact with the eyes or mouth, they are harmless to humans. Other frogs, however, will quickly die if kept in the same cage with a pickerel frog. That the secretions are a highly effective protection against enemies is proved by the fact that most snakes will not eat a pickerel frog.

Another handsomely colored and patterned North American species is the wood frog. This is essentially a frog of the more northern latitudes, occurring in Alaska, throughout much of Canada, and in the eastern United States. Its brown

Wood frog with the distinctive "robber's mask."

*The pig frog may grow
to over six inches long.*

and tan colors provide good concealment among the dead leaves of the forest floor; a distinctive feature is the "robber's mask," a dark patch extending backward from the eye. Moist wooded areas are the preferred habitat of this frog, which breeds in quiet woodland pools.

One of the largest North American frogs, but one with a very restricted range, is the pig frog of Florida, southern Texas, and South Carolina. As usual, it was the voice that gave the animal its name. A chorus of these frogs has been compared to a herd of swine grunting in unison—hardly a pleasant form of musical entertainment. Its size is approximately that of the bullfrog; the most easily recognizable difference between the two is the pig frog's much narrower and more pointed head.

Central and South America, the headquarters for tree frogs, have relatively few representatives of the genus *Rana*. Both the leopard and pickerel frogs occur in Central America, and similar species are found in the northern parts of South America.

By contrast, Asia has a considerable number of true frogs. Europe has not so very many, but some of them are very widespread and common species; the greatest number and variety of ranid frogs can be found in Africa.

The most common and therefore best-known frog of Europe is the edible frog, *Rana esculenta*. Its popular name

Common European grass, or edible, frog.

indicates that this was, and still is, the species widely hunted for man's dinner table. Records indicate that the legs of the edible frog and its close relatives, prepared in a variety of styles to tempt even the most jaded palate, were served at the opulent banquets of ancient Rome some two thousand and more years ago.

The edible frog is primarily aquatic, spending most of its life in the water or near the edge of the ponds, moats, or sluggish streams that are its habitat. Its favorite resting place by day is in the middle of a pond on a lily pad or a log, where it can watch for the flying insects that are captured in great and usually well-aimed leaps. It also often feeds under water on aquatic insects and small fish and can become a problem in fish hatcheries.

All kinds of flying insects plus beetles, worms, and insect larvae make up the bulk of its diet. Its green, black-spotted, and yellow-striped coloring blends well into its surroundings, and at the slightest sign of danger the frog leaps into the water and hides in the mud at the bottom.

The edible frog is just as enthusiastic a musician as his relatives. A large number of males in a pond will croak day and night during the breeding period, apparently engaged in a vocal endurance contest based on the principle of the more the merrier. The call sounds somewhat like the quacking of a hoarse duck. Although undoubtedly beautiful to their own ears, a solid week of uninterrupted croaking can produce short tempers and unflattering comments among the frogs' human neighbors.

The eggs of this species are deposited in tangled water plants. A single female may lay as many as ten thousand eggs in one season. Metamorphosis takes between three and four months, and the frogs then need two years to attain full maturity.

The other common frog of Europe is the grass frog. It resembles the North American wood frog in size and coloring, even including the dark "robber's mask." Also like its North American cousin the grass frog can survive in cold regions and at high altitudes. Thus it is found in Scandinavia, as well as high up in the Alps where the ponds and lakes are sometimes still covered with ice as late in the year as June. To make up for the short summer season in cold climates, the grass frog emerges much earlier from hibernation to breed, and its larvae complete their metamorphosis in a shorter time.

Southern Europe has a number of typical frogs such as the Grecian frog and Perez's frog. In appearance and habits they are very similar to the species described earlier and were in fact thought to be just different races, or subspecies, by older naturalists.

As mentioned before, Africa harbors a tremendous number of true frogs; the continent is distinguished by having many species of not only the type genus *Rana*, but also of several other genera, some of which are not found anywhere else in the world.

The life histories and habits of many African ranid frogs are hardly known. The apparently largely aquatic *Rana subsigillata* and the peculiar warty frog *Rana tuberculosa*, for example, are still being studied in order to establish exact knowledge about their life-styles.

The undisputed giant of the frog clan, or at least of those known to us, is the appropriately named *Rana goliath*, the giant

West African brown frog.

frog of the Belgian Congo. Its length has been recorded at ten inches but it is believed to attain a length of a foot or more. Not too much is known about the habits of this huge species. It lives in deep pools in the Congo River and is so shy that it is very difficult to capture. So far, the breeding habits of this frog, the length of its larval development, and the period of time needed to reach maturity are unknown.

The list of unusual African frogs is extensive. There is, for example, Gray's frog, *Rana grayi*, which provides the exception to the rule that the ranid frogs always deposit their eggs in the water. Gray's frog has found a way to make sure that its eggs can survive a period of drought during which many pools may dry out, killing all tadpoles that are not sufficiently developed. The eggs, which have an unusual hard outer covering, are deposited in damp soil above water level where they can absorb some moisture from their surroundings. The larvae can safely spend a few weeks inside during a dry spell. Then, when the first rains come and the pools fill, the tadpoles hatch from the eggs, wriggle out into the water, and complete their metamorphosis in the normal manner.

Gray's frog is not a stickler for an established routine. It seems to vary its habits according to prevailing conditions. Thus it has been found that females sometimes place their eggs in very deep water where the tadpoles have time to complete their metamorphosis without any danger of being left high and dry.

Gray's frog is much less aquatic than most of its relatives. Its hind feet are hardly webbed at all and it does not swim very well. It spends most of its life on land in tall grass and other vegetation that provides good cover.

One of the oddest members of the Ranidae is the peculiar hairy frog of the Cameroons. Hair on a frog may sound ridiculous, but during the breeding season the males of this species produce a growth resembling hair along their flanks and thighs. It is believed that these "hairs" are supplemental breathing organs that compensate for the much reduced lungs of this species and provide the additional oxygen needed for the increased metabolism during the breeding period. The females develop no such growth.

In addition to having the largest frog in the world, Africa also has what is perhaps the smallest—certainly one of the smallest—of all known frogs. *Phrynobatrachos chitialensis*, a pygmy with a big name, measures just one-half of an inch when grown. This mite lives in Nyasaland. A close relative, which measures a respectable three-quarters of an inch, is found in the Cape region of South Africa.

Frogs that live in the swift, rushing waters of mountain streams have problems not encountered by their relatives in calmer or standing waters. The chirping frog of South Africa, another dwarf species, has found a way to keep its eggs and larvae from being swept away by the swift currents. It deposits its eggs on damp moss, and the tadpoles hatch only after their hind legs have grown; then they wriggle about in the moss until the front legs grow also. A few days later the tail has been absorbed, and a froglet less than a quarter of an inch long is ready to face the world.

At the other end of the scale are the burrowing members of the family that live on the hot, dry plains of the continent. One of these, the cross-marked frog of South Africa, was discovered on a golf course almost by accident. These frogs are very secretive, remaining in their burrows throughout the day and coming out only at night. Such subterranean habits are necessary for frogs that have chosen as their habitat regions where it does not rain for nine months out of every year.

A very atypical member of the Ranidae is the golden

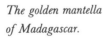

The golden mantella of Madagascar.

mantella of Madagascar. The entire body of this small frog, including the legs, is a beautiful golden orange, which is in startling contrast to the animal's large dark eyes. An inhabitant of wet forests, the mantella was long believed to be a member of a different family.

The Asian representatives of the Ranidae include a good many typical frogs such as the Indian bullfrog and the rice-paddy frog, but also quite a few unusual and strange-looking species. One of the latter is the dagger frog found in the highlands of Okinawa. This species is equipped with a weapon. With the exception of some South American frogs with teeth large enough to deliver a bite, no other salientian is armed with anything but its toxic secretions. The dagger frog, however, has long, well-developed thumbs ending in sharp spines. When captured it tries to grasp some part of its captor's body and drive the spines into the latter's flesh. The spines are sharp enough and the frog's strength is sufficient to draw blood from a man's hand.

Then there is *Rana adenopleura* from China, whose peculiar breeding habits warrant its inclusion in chapter seven. More typical are some aquatic members of the family found in rice paddies and pools over much of southern Asia and the islands of Malaysia. Excellent swimmers, they spend most of their life in the water and rarely visit dry land.

The exact opposites of these aquatic frogs can be found on New Guinea and Borneo. These species of the genus *Platymantis* prefer land over water to the extent that even the larvae complete their entire metamorphosis within the egg, which is deposited on damp ground. One handsome species from Borneo, *Platymantis boulengeri*, is a recent discovery.

The partial review of the main groups of frogs in this and the preceding chapter provides some idea of the wealth of diversity, both in physical attributes and in life-styles, that distinguishes the tailless amphibians. In the next two chapters, this diversity will be further underlined as we look at the remaining frog families and some individual species with peculiar habits.

6 Maverick Frog Families

In addition to the frogs described in the preceding chapters, there are a number of other groups, some very small and others sizeable, that include extremely interesting, colorful, and unusual species. Most of them are tropical and not widely known, but no review of the Salientia would be complete without a generous sampling of these families.

Although they comprise an array of very dissimilar-looking members, many species of the Leptodactylidae—literally, the weak-fingered ones—look very much like the typical frog or tree frog. Found mainly in the Americas but also in Australia, they are believed to be a very ancient frog family, and many are distinguished by peculiar habits.

The United States has only a few leptodactylids, most of them Central American species whose range barely extends into the extreme southern and southwestern parts of the country. There are, for example, the Mexican white-lipped frog and the Texas barking frog, both of which will be discussed later. A species originally introduced from Cuba is

The greenhouse frog; spotted phase.

the cute little greenhouse frog of southern Florida. The popular name of this inch-long immigrant refers to its inclination to take up residence in greenhouses. The tiny brownish frogs do not seem to mind the proximity of humans as long as they find shelter, moisture, and food. The eggs of this species are laid under damp debris, and metamorphosis takes place entirely within the egg. Having skipped the free-swimming larval stage, the greenhouse froglets hatch directly from the eggs with just a small tail stump still adhering to their bodies.

Some of the members of the type genus *Leptodactylus* are among the largest of the entire family—or, for that matter, of the entire order. Thus the handsomely colored South American bullfrog grows to a size of almost nine inches. During the breeding season, the male is attractively colored in shades of green, brown, and deep orange. Hunted by a host of predators including man, this frog is very shy and wary throughout its entire range, which includes much of Central and South America.

In appearance as well as in a very untypical pugnacity, some of the South American horned frogs of the genus *Ceratophrys*, which literally means horned brow, are not at all like other frogs. Many are protected by bony shields extending over the top of the head, and most have the peculiar triangular protuberances over the eyes that give the genus its name. These "horns"—prolongations of the upper eyelids—are soft flaps of skin and cannot do any harm. They do, however, lend the frogs a fierce expression, which happens to coincide with their disposition. They are fearless and aggressive and may attack creatures many times their size. They have large, dagger-shaped teeth in very strong and powerful upper jaws, lending their bite considerable emphasis. The unfroglike aggressiveness of the *Ceratophrys* species has given rise to a number of beliefs unsupported by fact. In Argentina, for instance, it is often claimed that a grazing animal, such as a horse or cow, will die if it is bitten on the lip by a horned frog. Horned frogs do not have a poisonous bite. The story probably has its origin in observed instances of horned frogs standing their ground against, and even attacking, creatures much larger than themselves.

Studies of the feeding habits of the horned frogs indicate not only an inclination toward cannibalism, but generally a preference for more substantial food than the insects, slugs, and worms that make up the main diet of most other frogs. Their strong jaws and often considerable size—the Amazonian *Ceratophrys cornuta* measures eight inches, and Boie's frog, *Ceratophrys boiei*, attains about the same length—suggests that, in addition to their own relatives, other vertebrates such as mice, young birds, and lizards form an important part of their diet.

Among the most peculiar members of the leptodactylids are certain aquatic species of a genus found only high up in the Andes, where they live in the icy waters of mountain lakes such as Lake Titicaca of Peru. The bodies of these frogs have become greatly modified as an adaptation to their aquatic existence. Tongue and teeth, needed by frogs that have to catch quick-moving insects, are lacking completely in these species. So are the lungs, which would serve no purpose for creatures that spend most of their lives at the bottom of lakes. In fact, lungs would only hamper them by forcing them to surface from time to time. The necessary oxygen is absorbed directly through the skin, which hangs loosely in great baggy folds around the bodies of these creatures, making them look as though they were wearing clothes several sizes too large for them. Removed from most of the survival problems that beset other frogs, they lead a rather inactive and sheltered life in their watery hideaways.

A large South American horned frog.

The exact opposite of these icy mountain waters is the dry, hot habitat preferred by leptodactylids that live in the desert areas of Australia. Because of the long dry spells, these frogs have to stay underground in burrows much of the time. Most of these rather toadlike species are nocturnal; an exception is the species known variously as the Catholic frog or the Holy Cross toad because of the cross-shaped pattern on its back. Since its food consists mainly of termites, it is often found in areas where rotting wood has attracted these insects.

Both the preceding species and the flat-headed frog of central Australia are distinguished by a most unusual ability which aids their survival in the hot, arid regions of their habitat. In addition to spending much of their time in moisture-conserving burrows, these frogs are capable of storing water in their bodies during the rainy period. This water, which gives them a bloated appearance, helps to sustain them through the dry season until the next rains come. Aborigines in these desert areas are known to dig up the flat-headed frogs and squeeze the water from their bodies for their own use.

The Catholic, or Holy Cross, frog of Australia.

A brightly colored corroboree toad. "Corroboree" is an Australian aborigine word meaning fiesta.

Two species of tailless amphibians are considered so different from all others that each had to be placed in a family of its own. One, called Darwin's frog, will be discussed in the next chapter because of its unique breeding habits. The other, the Mexican burrowing toad, is interesting to scientists because of certain anatomical features but has no exceptionally remarkable habits. It is a small, narrow-headed toad that lives in burrows and comes out to hunt only at night. Although its larva is somewhat peculiar-looking, it goes through a normal free-swimming stage.

Probably the most interesting of all the smaller families is the group known as the Dendrobatidae—literally, the tree climbers, but popularly called either the arrow-poison or poison-dart frogs. This group of generally small anurans includes many beautiful and brilliantly colored members. In addition, they have unusual breeding habits. Most intriguing to many people, however, is the fact that the skin secretions of these frogs is of such potent toxicity that South American Indians used the poison on the tips of hunting arrows and blowdarts. Animals wounded by such arrows are soon paralyzed and can then be easily captured. That the poison serves as a most effective defense against many predators seems to be borne out by the observation that the many species of arrow-poison frogs are abundant and rarely ever shy.

The type genus *Dendrobates* and the genus *Phyllobates* make up the majority of the family. They are found in the tropical forests of Central and South America. The colors of these frogs have to be seen to be believed. Live specimens sometimes exhibited in zoos look more like artificial objects than living creatures, with their glistening skins of incredible color combinations. Who would believe a shiny black frog with metallic blue spots? Or one whose equally shiny skin displays a dense pattern of bright red polka dots on a blue-black background? Others may have combinations of black or maroon with pink, chartreuse, green, and gold. The golden arrow-poison frog, only one and one-half inches long, has beautiful metallic hues of gold, green, and copper on all parts of its tiny body. Another exquisite species, although from a different genus, is the gold frog, a delicate creature only three-quarters of an inch long when fully grown. Its large black eyes contrast sharply with the golden-yellow color of its body.

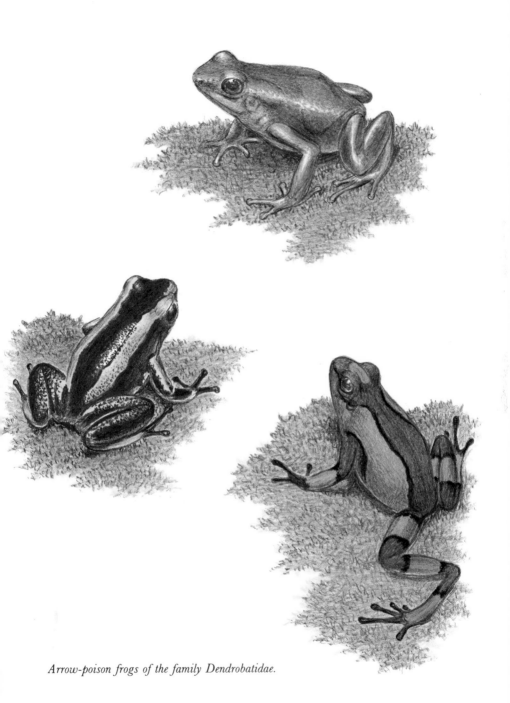

Arrow-poison frogs of the family Dendrobatidae.

Another mite, and probably the world's smallest frog, is *Sminthillus limbatus,* quite a mouthful for an elfin creature that attains an adult length of less than one-half of an inch! In addition to its special status as the tiniest member of the entire clan, it also has the distinction of being the only frog that lays just a single egg during each breeding season. This fact becomes truly incredible when viewed against the huge number of eggs produced by the majority of frog species. The female *Sminthillus* deposits this single, relatively large egg on damp ground in a protected location. The larva completes its metamorphosis inside and emerges as a fully developed froglet a little more than one-eighth of an inch long. Avoiding the hazardous free-swimming larval period is of course a necessary advantage for this species; whether some other factors add to its chances of survival is still unknown, but this appears likely, for despite its radical "birth-control" measures the tiny frog is not really rare and seems to be holding its own very well.

Similar to the dendrobatids in coloring and life-styles, and distributed over approximately the same range, are the Atelopodidae, the "imperfectly footed" ones. The family name refers to the fact that the inner toes may be missing and the outer toes fused in many species of this group. These frogs run to patterns of spots on a sharply contrasting background—black on yellow or orange, for instance, or bright green or red on black. From their unconcerned behavior, it may be assumed that they have relatively little to fear from natural enemies. Such fearlessness would seem to indicate that they, like the dendrobatids, have very toxic secretions "advertised" by their bright colors, and that this warning is heeded by a majority of predators.

With the exception of one or two species, a number of small families that have been variously shifted by scientists from one group of frogs to another are of interest mainly to those concerned with physiological detail. One interesting frog belonging to one of these families is the ghost frog of South Africa, a delicate creature less than three inches long. The light-colored skin of its underside is so thin and translucent that all its internal organs are visible. Additional unusual features of the ghost frog are tiny hooks in the skin of the forelegs and fingers and the diamond shape of the pupils of its eyes.

Another maverick is the paradoxical frog, a member of the Pseudidae, whose very name indicates the trouble this particular group has caused scientists who have tried to classify it correctly. *Pseudis paradoxa* of northern South America got its name from the disproportionate size of the tadpole compared to that of the adult frog. Although some rather small frogs may have relatively large tadpoles, the size of the adult can usually be estimated from the size of the larva in advanced stages of development. Not in the case of the paradoxical frog, however, for the tadpole of this three-inch species may measure over ten inches long! This means that the normal process of growth in the last stages of metamorphosis is reversed, and a shrinkage in body size has to take place in order to bring the tadpole down to adult size.

Until fairly recently, naturalists included among the tree frogs an interesting and colorful group found in Africa, Madagascar, and parts of southeastern Asia. In outward appearance, including the distinctive toe disks, these species do indeed strongly resemble tree frogs. Some live high in the treetops and are nimble climbers and jumpers. However, certain anatomical details have led scientists to believe that unlike the tree frogs, these species did not evolve from toads, but rather from the more advanced true frogs. Like many frog families, they have no popular name; their scientific designation Rhacophoridae, which replaced an older term referring to their jumping abilities, is based upon physiological features. The rhacophorids are a large family numbering several hundred species.

Some of the African members especially have prominent and often brilliant color patterns. Some of the so-called sedge frogs of the genus *Hyperolius* look almost unreal with their contrasting patterns of stripes and spots that may feature emerald green, orange, and scarlet, often in combinations with white and black.

One member with less brilliant colors but a very interesting life-style is the tiny arum frog. Only an inch long, and usually ivory white, this delicate little creature has chosen a romantic habitat: the center of the white blossoms of the arum

The silver-lined sedge frog.

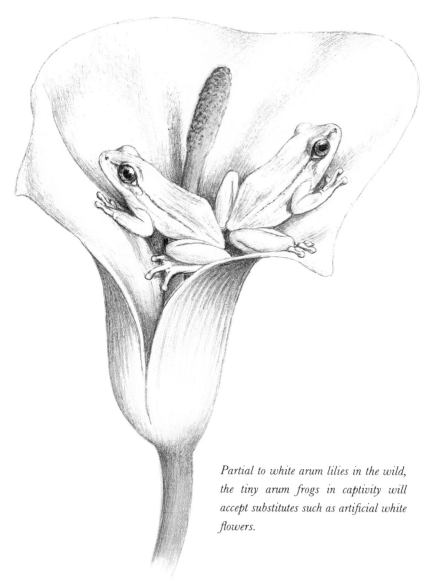

Partial to white arum lilies in the wild, the tiny arum frogs in captivity will accept substitutes such as artificial white flowers.

swamp lily. Several of these little frogs may be found nestling in one of the cup-shaped flowers, where they remain for as long as the lilies are in bloom. Once that period is past, however, they have to move out, and with their change of lodging they change their color. The ivory white is replaced by a dark brown with lighter greenish or silvery stripes along the sides, and once again they blend into the color scheme of the now blossomless vegetation. Next season's bloom brings back the ivory hues.

Behavior contrary to that known from all other frogs is displayed by the African gray tree frog, an interesting species not closely related to the North American hylid of that name. Although it is difficult to imagine a frog that dislikes getting wet, such a unique repugnance is precisely one of the outstanding features of this frog's behavior. With the coming of the first rains of the wet season, the frog moves out of its habitual haunts and into some dry place. In order to escape the wetness outside it frequently even invades houses. How these animals manage to keep their skin moist even in very hot and dry weather is still puzzling to observers. Equally intriguing are the breeding habits of this species.

In Asia, a few frogs of the type genus *Rhacophorus* have been credited with being able to fly. This, of course, is not true. Birds and bats are the only vertebrates capable of true flight. However, certain species, such as the Malaysian flying frog and the Japanese gliding frog, can make tremendous flying leaps that may carry them a distance of forty or fifty feet at a downward angle. They are aided in these "parachute" jumps by the large webs between fingers and toes, which they spread wide and stiffly during their leaps. They are also aided by their light build and their ability to make their bodies concave while in the air.

The last important family outside the main groups is that comprising the narrow-mouthed toads. The Microhylidae occur in practically all parts of the world with the exception only of Australia and Europe. These highly specialized frogs are not as often seen as most others of their kind because they have secretive, nocturnal habits and spend much of their time underground in burrows. As a matter of fact, some have chosen to live permanently in anthills and termites' nests, which assures them comfortable lodging as well as an abundant and easily accessible food supply. Those who may wonder about the comforts of living in an anthill may rest assured that these narrow-mouthed toads, which are immune to the bites of their enraged hosts, find their quarters extremely convenient and satisfactory.

As their popular name indicates, the most distinctive characteristic of these toads is the very narrow mouth, which of course limits them to prey not exceeding the size of the ants and termites most of them favor. Their heads are small, and many have a pointed snout and a lateral fold of skin across the back of the head.

A narrow-mouthed toad.

Several species of Microhylidae occur throughout the southern and southwestern regions of the United States. One is the eastern narrow-mouthed toad, which may be found from Maryland to Florida and Texas. Another is the Mexican narrow-mouthed toad, popularly known as the sheep frog because of its bleating call. It ranges from Texas into Mexico and looks much like its eastern relative except for a yellow streak down its back and some light lines on the underside.

Other members occur in South America and especially in Asia and Africa, which harbor the most attractive species of this group. A good example is the Asiatic painted frog of Malaysia and southern China, with its pattern of raspberry pink and chocolate brown.

The species of the African genus *Breviceps*, which means short-headed and is very descriptive, are little frogs with pug noses, small heads, and fat, puffed-up bodies—veritable caricatures of a frog. They cannot swim and never enter the water.

African short-headed frog, popularly called rain frog.

Their larvae also have no free-swimming phase and hatch from the egg as fully formed froglets. One species with a claim to fame is the South African rain frog, so called because the natives of the regions where it occurs believe that it can influence droughts and bring much-needed rain. For that reason, they take great care never to harm the little creatures whenever they come across them. This, then, is at least one frog that has nothing to fear from the humans it encounters in its habitat—unless, of course, they happen to be scientists on a collecting trip.

The generally less well known frogs described in the preceding pages are living proof of the great diversity found in this order, a diversity which will be further underlined by the peculiar breeding habits of many species described in the next chapter.

7 Unusual Breeding Habits

In any large group of animals, there are always some that do not fit into the behavior patterns typical of the majority. Sometimes they are distinguished by having retained some primitive features reminiscent perhaps of long-gone ancestral types. In other instances they may have developed highly specialized and sophisticated habits that set them apart from the rest of their group. Most often these differences are expressed in the various aspects of breeding habits such as courtship and brood-care performances. Among birds, for example, the megapodes, or brush turkeys, have retained the reptilian method of burying their eggs in mounds of sand and rotting vegetation and then letting the sun and the warmth generated by the decaying organic material do the job of incubating. At the other end of the scale, we find the devoted and long-lasting care many birds give their young, as well as the highly specialized courtship behavior of species such as the Australian bowerbirds, whose males build special "love nests."

These bowers serve for courtship activities only. After mating, the female goes off on her own to build the nest that will house the eggs and young.

There is a popular tendency to believe that care for the young becomes more pronounced as animals progress upward on the evolutionary ladder. This is only partially true. Practically no reptile, for instance, cares in any way for its offspring once the eggs have been laid. Among amphibians, which rank below reptiles, there are quite a few instances of specialized breeding care, and the same is true for fish, some of which have developed highly sophisticated types of breeding behavior.

The rule among amphibians is of course a complete lack of brood care. The eggs, usually in great numbers, are deposited and fertilized, then each parent goes its own way. The development of the young is left to chance—which means that most of them become easy prey for predators even before, or shortly after, they hatch from the eggs. In view of this typical behavior, those among the frogs that deviate from it are especially interesting. Also of interest is the observation that brood care is found among the most primitive as well as among the most advanced types of the order. Thus males of Hochstetter's frog—one of the most primitive species known— were observed guarding the eggs after the females had deposited them on the wet floor of small cracks and crevices moistened by the seepage of mountain springs.

Much more astonishing, however, is the performance of the earlier-mentioned Surinam toad, also a primitive species. The brood care of this frog requires the active participation of the male as well as the female, for after the eggs have been fertilized, the male laboriously pushes them up and onto the female's back where the skin is thickened. After the several dozen eggs have been thus deposited, the male, his part of the job done, returns to his normal way of life. Within a few hours,

A Surinam toad with eggs that are ready to hatch; one young toad is emerging.

European male midwife toad
carrying eggs.

the skin on the female's back swells and encloses the eggs completely. From then on and for the next few weeks, the mother carries the developing embryos securely enveloped in the skin of her back. In this way they are protected against the myriad of enemies that normally beset amphibian eggs and larvae. Then, one day, one tiny lid of skin after another pops open on the mother's back, and out of each little pocket a fully developed toadlet emerges and swims off.

Probably the most famous of all amphibians that practice brood care is a species whose habits were recorded at a much earlier date than those of some less accessible exotic kinds. This is the European midwife toad. Despite its name, however, it is the male that bears the burden of caring for the offspring.

Midwife toads, unlike most others of their kind, mate on land. The eggs—usually several dozen of them—are relatively long and are produced in strings that look like a row of beads. As soon as the male has fertilized them, he starts to push his hind legs through the egg mass, and continues to do so until he has succeeded in winding the strings tightly around his thighs. During the daytime, the male now stays in an underground burrow. At night, he comes out to search for food and at the same time dampens the eggs in the dew.

For a period of about four weeks, the male carries the eggs about in this fashion. Finally, he seems to know instinctively that the time has come for the tadpoles to emerge; entering the nearest pond or large pool, he waits until all the eggs have hatched and the tadpoles, which are already in an advanced stage of metamorphosis, have swum off. Now his duties are completed, and he can go back to his normal way of life.

Another devoted father is the male Texas barking frog, the only North American species known to practice any type of brood care. This toadlike frog, whose voice sounds somewhat like the yapping of a terrier, is native to the American southwest, living in cracks and crevices where it can find the moisture it needs to survive. The young develop completely inside the egg without a free-swimming stage. The female deposits her eggs in some moisture-holding crevice and abandons them. The male stays nearby after fertilizing them and guards them during the next four or five weeks until the froglets emerge. Even more important than the father's guard duties is the fact that he moistens the eggs with his urine whenever they become too dry.

Opened and greatly enlarged egg of the barking frog showing fully developed tadpole inside.

*Darwin's frog, a peculiar
mouthbreeding species.*

One of the most bizarre types of amphibian brood care is practiced by the male of a species that has the distinction of having been placed into a family all by itself. This is the mouthbreeding frog, *Rhinoderma darwinii*, named after Charles Darwin, who discovered it during his travels in South America. A small creature attaining a length of just over an inch, Darwin's frog, also locally called the "vaquero" in Argentina, provides a unique dwelling for its young during their larval development: the vocal sac of the male.

The first phase of the peculiar breeding behavior begins with several males gathering about a clutch of eggs laid by a single female. After the attendant males have collectively fertilized the eggs, they stay nearby waiting for the moment— about three weeks later—when the embryos begin to move inside the eggs and are close to hatching. At that point, each waiting male scoops up several eggs in his mouth and, with the help of his tongue, maneuvers them into his enlarged vocal sac, which extends all the way back to the groin, then turns up, over, and forward until it reaches the chin. Stretched out to its full length, the vocal sac thus would be almost twice the frog's body length.

For several weeks following their transferal to the vocal sac, the young tadpoles grow and complete their metamorphosis securely tucked away inside the body of the male—who may or may not be their own father! Their presence does not interfere with his taking food, although they start pressing against his internal organs and his skeletal structure as they grow, sometimes to the extent that the pelvic girdle is dislocated. However, soon after the young emerge from the male's mouth as fully developed froglets with only tiny tails adhering to their bodies, the male's anatomy quickly adjusts itself and everything goes back to normal.

In view of the fact that the young of Darwin's frog are raised in the males' vocal sacs, the term "mouthbreeding" is somewhat inaccurate for that species. There is, however, a frog found in equatorial Africa that truly deserves being called the mouthbreeding frog. The female of *Hylambates brevirostris* is a devoted mother who foregoes nourishment in order to care for her young. As soon as her eggs, which are relatively few, have been fertilized, she gathers them up in her mouth and keeps them there for the entire duration of the metamorphosis. This makes it impossible for her to eat, and she becomes visibly thinner toward the end of her long fast. However, she thereby gives her young the best possible protection during the most critical stages of their life, and when they emerge from her mouth as fully developed froglets, they have a headstart matched by only a few other species.

It is not so very often that outstanding physical attributes and exceptional behavior are found in the same animal. The South American arrow-poison frogs are examples of such a combination. As we have already seen, these frogs have

Male arrow-poison frog carrying
his young on his back.

brilliant and often very beautiful color patterns. They also
possess extremely toxic secretions that have given rise to their
collective name. In addition, they are also distinguished by
practicing a form of brood care that has been described as
"baby-sitting." The male carries his young around on his back
until they are in an advanced state of metamorphosis. In order
to do this the male attaches the eggs to his back after he has
fertilized them. Unlike those of the Surinam toad, however,
the tadpoles of the arrow-poison frogs are not enclosed in skin
pockets or depressions. When the young hatch, they just ride

on their father's back, managing to hang on until they reach a certain point in their development and are ready to be on their own. The male seems to sense this moment, for he enters the water and thereby gives his young a chance to get off his back and swim away.

Backpacking the young appears to be a rather fashionable method of brood care among amphibians. There are several different types of backpacking, mainly among South American frogs. One of the most sophisticated types is the skin pouch of the marsupial frog. The German name for this species is *Taschenfrosch*, which means pocket frog. The female carries her eggs in her pouch, which extends over her entire back. As the young grow, she begins to look grotesquely swollen and top-heavy. When the froglets are ready to emerge, she pulls the slit of the pouch open with her hind foot, so that the very delicate and fragile young will have no difficulty in getting out.

Male and female marsupial frogs. The male is not only smaller than the female, it also lacks the pouch in which the eggs develop.

Female Goeldi's frog "backpacking" her eggs.

Other South American tree frogs with a variation of the piggy-back type of brood care are the species of the genus *Flectonotus*, which have no popular names. One could say that these females put all their eggs in one basket, for on their backs they have a basket-like depression surrounded by an elevated rim. Each female lays fewer than two dozen eggs—a small number when compared to that of most other frog species—and places them in this basket. When the tadpoles hatch from the eggs, they are already far advanced, having grown hind legs. The female then unloads them in rainwater that has collected at the base of large leaves of certain air plants. It then takes only a few more days for the tadpoles to complete their metamorphosis in their nurseries high above ground.

Although not breeding behavior in the strict sense, the method of reproduction found among toads of the genus *Nectophrynoides* is so strange for amphibians, and the means by which they manage it so mysterious, that it warrants inclusion in this chapter. The few species of this genus are the only ones among the approximately twenty-five hundred different kinds of anurans that bear their young alive. How the sperm is introduced into the female's body we do not know, for no copulatory organ has been found in the male. Exactly how the tadpoles develop in the mother's uterus has not yet been established either. It is believed that the tadpoles' long, slender tails—useless for locomotion inside the female's body—are instrumental in providing the young with additional oxygen via contact with the uterine walls. Until further research yields additional information, the why and how of this group's manner of reproduction is an intriguing mystery.

Nest building is so rare among frogs that most people do not know that nest-building frogs exist. The South American smith frog mentioned spends considerable energy on fashioning a nest for its young. This nest looks like a miniature

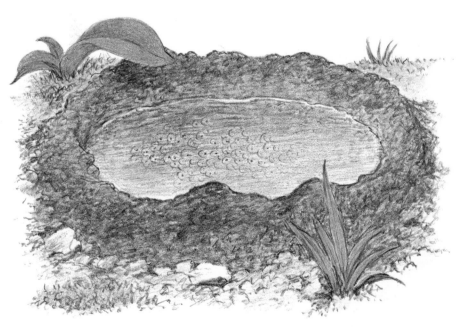

Mud nest with eggs of the South American smith frog.

crater, with a rim of mud surrounding a bowl-shaped center with just enough water in it to comfortably cover the eggs. The nest is about a foot across and is located at the edge of a pool; its rim is just high enough to be above water level. This means that the first rain after the tadpoles have hatched will flood the nest and wash them into deeper water. Until then, however, eggs and hatchlings will be kept safe from aquatic predators at a very critical period of their lives.

Another mud nest is made by *Rana adenopleura* of China. The males dig holes into the soft soil at the edge of a pool. Then they all call in unison until a female appears, at which time the courtship call is replaced by a very different, low note. Only after the female has chosen a mate do the rest of the males switch back to the original courtship chorus designed to attract other females. The eggs are deposited in the mud hole dug by the male, where they are safe from attacks by aquatic insects.

Quite another type of "nest" is the mass of frothy foam produced by the females of certain species from a fluid discharged together with the eggs. Members of different families are known for such foam nests; thus Guenther's frog, a South American leptodactylid, and the Mexican white-lipped frog both provide this type of protective envelope for their eggs. Among the Rhacophoridae, the most sophisticated and elaborate foam nest is produced by the African gray tree frog, the species mentioned earlier for its unique dislike of wetness. This largely arboreal frog chooses as a breeding location a tree or bush directly over a water hole. As the eggs are laid, the female produces the mucous secretion which both parents beat into a thick frothy foam with their hind legs until it looks something like beaten egg whites. The eggs are located at the center of this froth, whose outer layers are soon baked into a hard crust wherever they are exposed to the air. In order to prevent the foam from hardening too much and thereby killing the young, the mother remains on the foam nest for several days, embracing it so that her body covers most of the upper surface. As the tadpoles hatch, their weight makes them sink to the bottom of the nest, where they finally fall into the water below as the crust breaks and releases them.

From the preceding parade of frogs of every type—the primitive and the advanced, the typical and the extraordinary, the aquatic and the arboreal—one fact emerges clearly. There are very few animal groups that combine so many fascinating physical and behavioral features with so many traits beneficial to man as the frogs and toads of the world.

Bibliography

Ahl, Ernst. *Das Tierreich, Anura III.* Berlin and Leipzig: De Gruyter, 1931.

Cochran, Doris M. *Living Amphibians of the World.* New York: Doubleday, 1961.

——. "Our Friend the Frog." *National Geographic,* vol. 61, no. 5 (1932).

Oliver, J. A. *The Natural History of North American Amphibians.* Princeton, N.J.: Van Nostrand, 1955.

Rose, Walter. *The Reptiles and Amphibians of Southern Africa.* Capetown: Maskew Miller, 1950.

Schmidt, Karl P. *A Checklist of North American Amphibians and Reptiles.* Chicago: American Society of Ichthyologists and Herpetologists, 1953.

Van Kampen, P. N. *The Amphibians of the Indo-Australian Region.* Leiden: Brill, 1923.

Waite, Edgar R. *The Reptiles and Amphibians of South Australia.* Adelaide: Weir, 1929.

Zim, H. S., and Smith, H. M. *Reptiles and Amphibians: A Guide to Familiar American Species.* New York: Simon and Schuster, 1953.

Zwarenstein, H., Sapeika, N., and Shapiro, H. A. *Xenopus laevis: A Bibliography.* Capetown: African Bookman, 1940.

Index of Scientific Names
of Species Illustrated

(In Order of Appearance)

123

Index

125